Acknowledgments

I have many people to thank for the publication of this book! First, I wish to acknowledge my husband and best friend, Brett, who has always been so supportive and insightful. I am grateful for our two talented children, Kelsie and Colter, for their continued love and involvement in our lives out here on Vancouver Island. I wish to dedicate this book to our three wonderful grandchildren – Kiera, Charlotte and Zackary, for their zest for life and their love of the natural environment. A big thank you also goes out to my two loving and creative sisters, Barb and Claire, for their encouragement. I am also indebted to the Vancouver Island Elder College program for their continued dedication to lifelong learning and their support of the courses I teach for them. I wish to acknowledge the invaluable experiences and talented people I worked with during my career with the two Calgary School Boards in Alberta.

I wish to thank my photographer, Nicole Ferguson, for being such a capable person and wonderful person to work with. Although not connected with this book, her work with VIU Elder College has been appreciated by all the instructors who have volunteered to pass on their love of learning and knowledge to those who are 'fifty or better'. Finally, I appreciate the efforts and patience of Amazon Publishing in the completion of this book. Thank you, everyone!

Terri Bowen

Lighthouse Country's Oceanside Alphabet

Terri Bowen

Amazingly arid arbutus

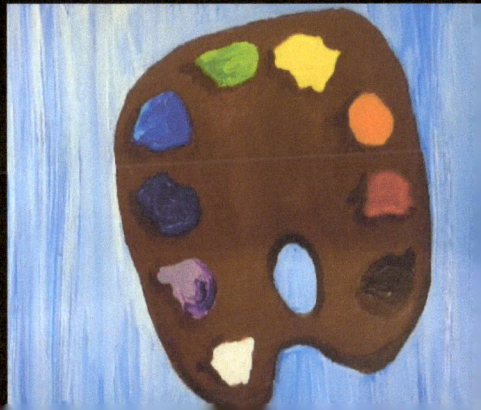

Big beautiful beaches

Crawling crusty crabs

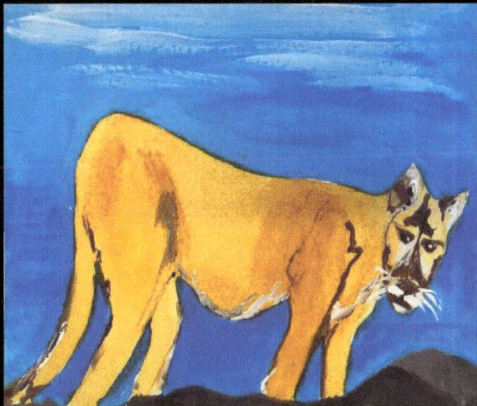

Darting deer and dragonflies

Elegant elevated eagles

Fantastic flora and fauna

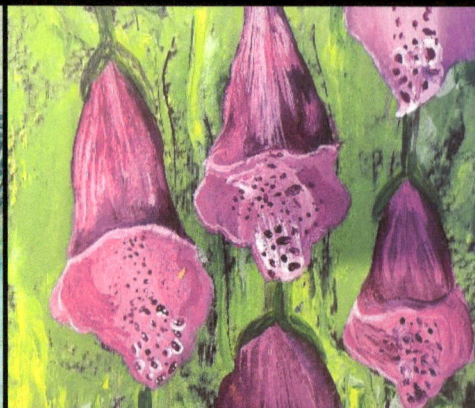

Giant geese and goslings

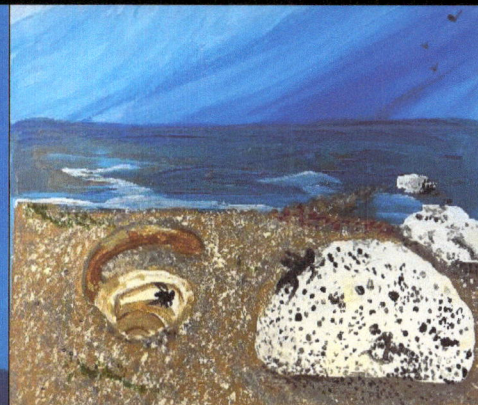

Hauntingly hazy hillsides

Interesting inching insects

Jiggly jittery jellyfish

Kite-like kestrels

Luckily lit lighthouses

Monstrous munching millipedes

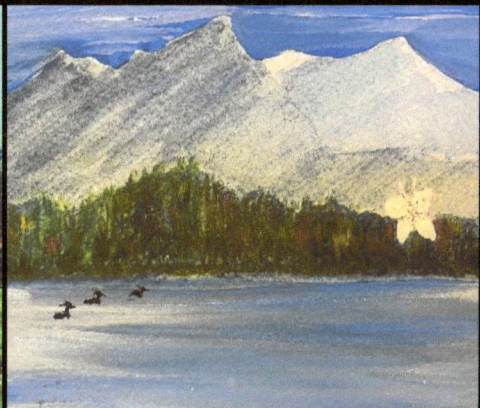

Nettle filled nook-like nests

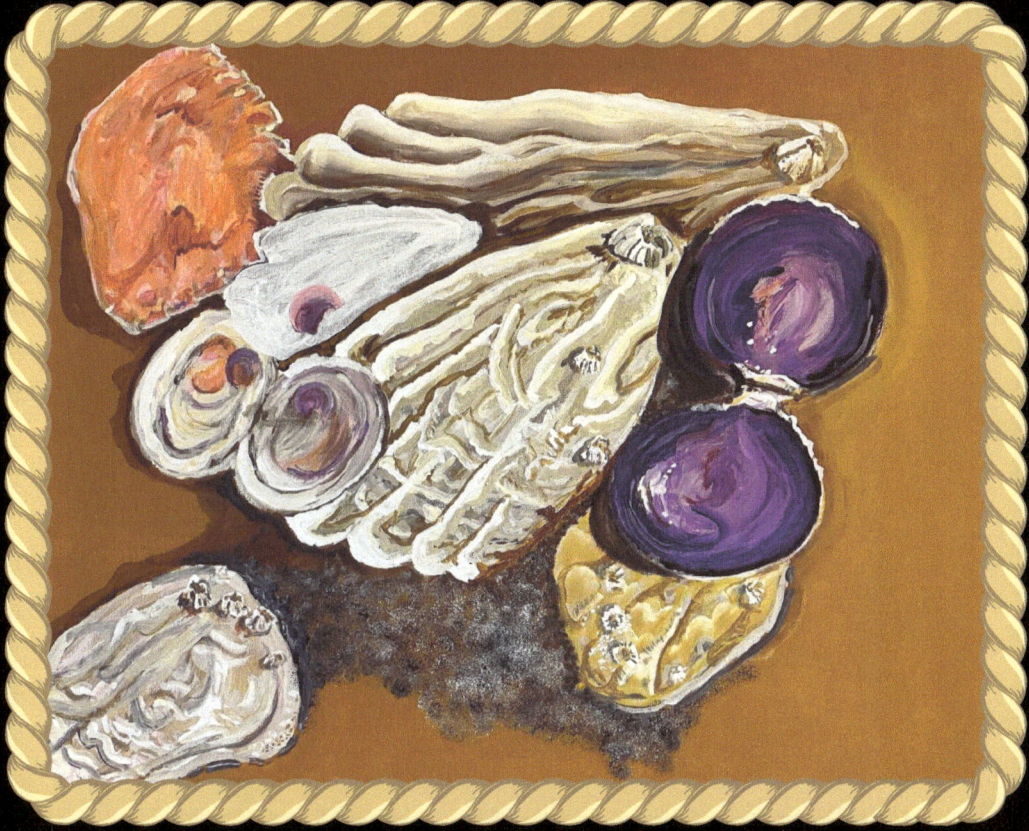

Oversized oval oysters

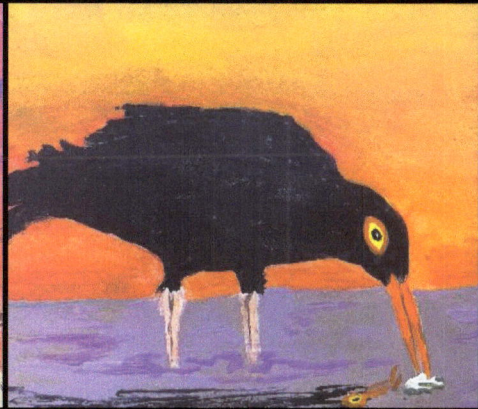

Peaceful Pacific panoramas

Quick quiet quests

Rapidly rushing rivers

Sleepy silky sea lions

Towering tent-like trees

Unique unbelievable urchins

Vast vivid vistas

Wild wetland waterfowl

Xciting xiting Xiphosura

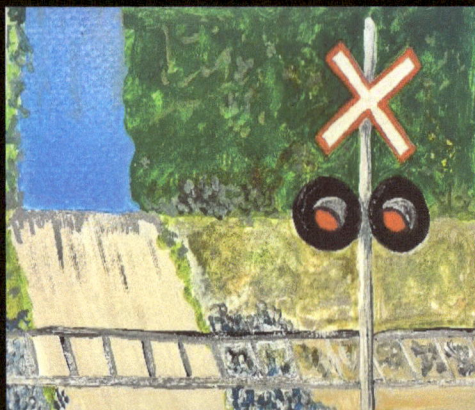

Yawning yellow yarrow

Zippy zenith zones

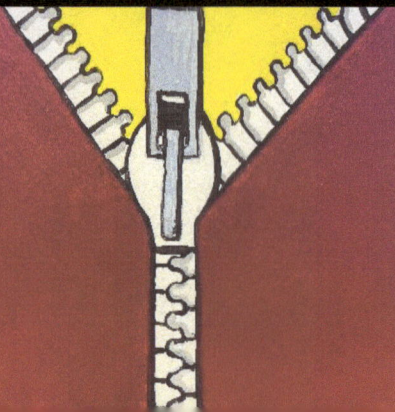

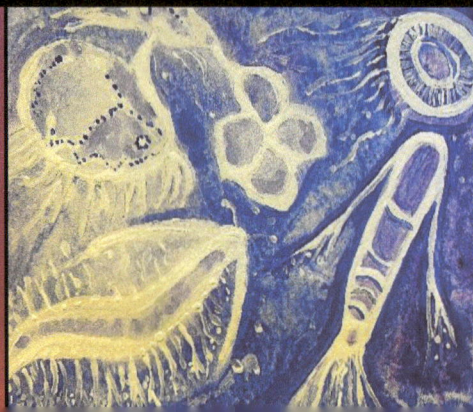

Can you remember which picture goes with what letter? (Hint, there are two letters missing.)

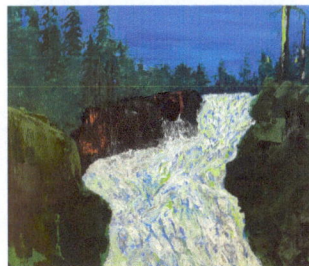

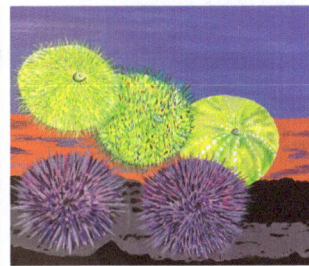

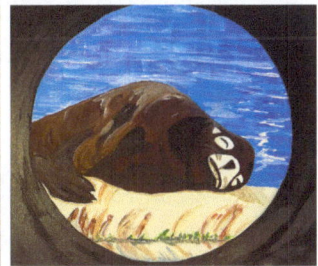

Glossary for Lighthouse Country's Oceanside Alphabet

Author's Note: The flora, fauna and activities contained in this glossary are only but a tiny portion of the fantastic environment of Lighthouse Country and Oceanside on Vancouver Island. Have fun thinking of your own ideas that match each letter!

A: Aphid, Arbutus, Artists, Auk, Azalea

B: Beach, Bear, Bee, Brant, Butterfly Bush

C: Chickadee, Clam, Cormorant, Cougar, Crab

D: Dahlia, Deer, Dipper, Dolphin, Dove, Dragonfly, Driftwood

E: Eagle, Easel, Echinacea, Eider Duck, Elk

F: Family's Future, Fern, Fish, Fledgling Falcon's Feather, Flicker, Foxglove, Frog, Fruit

G: Golden Eye Duck, Gooey Duck, Goose (Canada), Goslings, Granite, Grasshopper, Gull

H: Halibut, Harlequin Duck, Heron, Hills, Hummingbird, Happiness

I: Ice Cream, Igneous Rock, Inchworm, Ink Cap (mushroom), Island (Vancouver)

J: Jay (Steller's), Jellyfish, Joe Pye Weed, Junco

K: Kayak, Kestrel, Kingbird, Kingfisher, Kite

L: Ladybug, Lighthouse, Lizard, Loon, Lupine

M: Marmot, Merganser, Millipede, Moth, Mountains, Mushroom

N: Nest, Nighthawk, Nooks, Nutcracker, Nuthatch,

O: Ocean, Orca, Otter (River), Oyster, Oyster Catcher

P: Painted Turtle, Panorama, Pebbles, Pintail Duck, Pterosaur

Q: Quail, Qualicum (Salmon), Queen Anne's Lace, Quest, Quill, Quilt

R: Rabbit, Racoon, Raspberry, Raven, Rhododendron, Rudbeckia

S: Scoter, Sea Lion, Seastar ('Starfish'), Sand, Snake

T: Teal, Toad, Trees, Trillium, Trumpeter Swan

U: Ukulele, Umbrella, Ursus Major (The Big Dipper)

V: Vegetables, Violet, Vista, Vulture

W: Warbler, Water, Waterfowl, Wetland, Worms

X: Xanthophyl, Zenolith, X-ing, Xiphosura (Horseshoe Crab), Xylography (wood cuts and engravings)

Y: Yacht, Yarrow, Yellow Legs, Yoga

Z: Zephyr, Zipper, Zenith, Zone and finally, Zygote

About the Author

Terri is a certified expert handwriting analyst which causes some people to just type their notes to her now rather than write them! She has spoken in several venues in Calgary and in Lighthouse Country on the topics of Graphology (analysis of handwriting/printing traits) and Graphotherapy (changing certain traits in your handwriting to achieve greater success in life). But her passion has become her art....

Winner of several Grand Aggregate Arts Awards from the Lighthouse County Fair, Terri has had a camera in hand ever since Santa gave her a black and white Kodak Brownie for Christmas in 1962. Terri went on to shoot 1000's of pictures in the various Calgary schools she taught at, with some of these being printed in the dozens of school yearbooks she published. Her teaching adventures and misadventures began in 1975 and ended in December of 2008 when she retired as a principal of a Learning Through the Arts School and came out here to live and dream with her husband, Brett, in beautiful Lighthouse Country.

During the 30-plus years of teaching, Terri facilitated school divisions, individual schools and her writing clubs to publish dozens of illustrated student writing anthologies of poetry and short stories. Her largest club of 130 elementary students had their book placed in several libraries in Calgary. Her last poetry/painting book, published by her Grade 4 writing club, was entitled "I Want to Go Where the Wild Flowers Grow", which was recognized as one of the top 10 in Canada in Scholastic's "KidsCanWrite" competition. Terri is currently working on other illustrated books when she's not out volunteering, kayaking, biking or taking pictures of clouds and sunsets.

Mrs. Bowen (like the island!) works in many mediums although she is primarily a painter and jewelry designer. She currently teaches several Art courses through Vancouver Island's Elder College and North Island College. Terri has painted many murals including a 360 degree mural of Alberta's energy sources and flora/fauna at her last school and a West Coast forest scene at Munchkinland in Qualicum Beach. Her art has been featured in The Old

School House calendar, celebrating the participants of the Qualicum Beach Grand Prix Art contest. You can also enjoy her colorful banners hanging down at the popular wharf walk in old town Nanaimo. Terri does murals and commission work, transferring photos into large exciting watercolours and acrylics. Her passion is to travel the world to see famous galleries and museums. She also finds there is never a dull moment out here on Vancouver Island.

www.ingramcontent.com/pod-product-compliance
Lightning Source LLC
Chambersburg PA
CBHW061157030426

42337CB00002B/31